SHADOWGRAPH

Mary Burritt
Christiansen
Poetry Series

MARY BURRITT CHRISTIANSEN POETRY SERIES
Hilda Raz | Series Editor

The Mary Burritt Christiansen Poetry Series publishes two to four books a year that engage and give voice to the realities of living, working, and experiencing the West and the Border as places and as metaphors. The purpose of the series is to expand access to, and the audience for, quality poetry, both single volumes and anthologies, that can be used for general reading as well as in classrooms.

Also available in the Mary Burritt Christiansen Poetry Series:

Crosscut: A Trail Crew Memoir in Poems by Sean Prentiss
The Music of Her Rivers: Poems by Renny Golden
to cleave: poems by Barbara Rockman
After Party: Poems by Noah Blaustein
The News as Usual: Poems by Jon Kelly Yenser
Gather the Night: Poems by Katherine DiBella Seluja
The Handyman's Guide to End Times: Poems by Juan J. Morales
Rain Scald: Poems by Tacey M. Atsitty
A Song of Dismantling: Poems by Fernando Pérez
Critical Assembly: Poems of the Manhattan Project by John Canaday

For additional titles in the Mary Burritt Christiansen Poetry Series, please visit unmpress.com.

University of New Mexico Press   Albuquerque

james cihlar

THE SHADOWGRAPH *poems*

Library of Congress Cataloging-in-Publication Data

Title   The shadowgraph: poems / James Cihlar.

Description   First edition. | Albuquerque: University of New Mexico
Press, 2020. | Series: Mary Burritt Christiansen poetry series |
Includes bibliographical references.

Identifiers   LCCN 2019032059 (print) | LCCN 2019032060 (e-book) |
ISBN 9780826361257 (paperback) | ISBN 9780826361264 (e-book)

Subjects   LCGFT: Poetry.

Classification   LCC PS3603.I356 S53 2020 (print) |
LCC PS3603.I356 (e-book) | DDC 811/.6—dc23

LC record available at https://lccn.loc.gov/2019032059

LC e-book record available at https://lccn.loc.gov/2019032060

James Cihlar is a fiscal year 2017 recipient
of an Artist Initiative grant from the Minnesota
State Arts Board. This activity is funded, in part,
by the Minnesota State Legislature from the State's
arts and cultural heritage fund with money
from the vote of the people of Minnesota on
November 4, 2008.

Cover illustration   *Mandala–Concentric Space*, 1970, by
Clarence Holbrook Carter, Sheldon Museum of Art, University
of Nebraska–Lincoln, Gift of Peat, Marwick, Mitchell & Co.,
U-3663.1985. Photo © Sheldon Museum of Art.

Cover author photo   Brad Stauffer

Cover and text design   Mindy Basinger Hill

Composed in Minion Pro and Chypre Ext Book

FOR VIKKI, RITA, JULIE, AND KATHLEEN

CONTENTS

THE SHADOWGRAPH

MARWYCK

"I wear myself out keeping myself calm."
— *Barbara Stanwyck*

I can love them all, now,
because what does it matter?
A chemical in the brain
makes time spin faster.
The rolling wheel of aftermath
loses heat as it tumbles
down the dell.

A Christmas card
my mother bought
is my memory palace,
all the elves asleep
in a row of beds
on a travertine balcony
above the hearth.

Let's pin it down
to blueprints. How much
closer can we get to living?
Stanwyck built a castle
in the Southern California desert
and made it look like
Camelot.

She rode the train
from Hollywood
to seventy years ago.
When FDR pressed a button
in the White House,
confetti rained down
on Omaha.

I bet God will understand
the smallness of my wants.
In the middle of summer
I miss summer.
Marwyck will be my heaven.
I've peopled it already
with ghosts of the living.

SATURDAY NIGHT

A cream square framed by a white border stamped DEC • 73.
Perspective as flat as a Grandma Moses painting,
my older sister's head in lower left inaccurately small—

the honey-blonde grain of one long wing of hair curtaining
the vertical line of her profile, with outsized right hand crabbed
in foreground, the tip of her ring finger obscured by her lips.

*When Carol Burnett tugs her ear, she's telling
her grandmother she's okay*, my sister said.
My grandmother's legs enter the frame mid-left,

the pink-and-cream circle of her knee in floral pajamas
superimposed on the grid of red and green squares behind.
Tentatively reaching into the frame just above,

a lone Christmas tree branch, red ball hanging at the tip.
Against a field of silver lace, gray wallpaper, and beige door,
I'm curled impossibly into a lavender upholstered rocker,

which I almost swear I bought secondhand twenty years later
as the first piece for my apartment in a different city.
Center frame is my younger brother, his arms around the dog.

We all stare off frame to the right at an implied screen,
perhaps at Mary Tyler Moore's name multiplying,
my mother laughing, *Doesn't she remind you of me?*

Or even better, the crescendo of horns and drums
of a CBS Special Presentation, as a rainbow
spirals out at me from a field of black.

RETROSPECTIVE

Midnight in the middle of summer,
too hot to sleep,
my mother pulled the bedroom curtain aside

to reveal what I thought
was always out there: a kaleidoscope of eyes,
giant moths filling the pane, no two alike,

a reverse glass painting in shades of brown,
each pair of wings a set of eyes,
hundreds of moths pressing themselves

against the glass
until no bare space was left,
their wings unblinking, looking in.

This happens when we close our eyes,
she said. They come looking for something
that's not here.

We don't have the words to describe,
so we can't do anything
but keep the curtain closed

and know they are there.
That's how she taught me about memory,
an eye above my head.

THE STRAND THEATER

on West Broadway and Seventh in Council Bluffs,
Iowa, was refurbished in 1927 from an opera house
to a movie palace. In the sixties my mother would drop off my sisters
and me on a Saturday afternoon, unsupervised, to watch
matinees of *Support Your Local Sheriff* or *Cat Ballou*,
The Man Called Flintstone or *Hey There, It's Yogi Bear!*
Approved by but absent of my mother,
the Strand was independence in childhood. My mother's
presence hovered nevertheless, in the
painted tapestries that adorned the walls of classical women
performing enigmatic tasks, or in the sculptures of goddesses
ready to step from their pedestals and circle the
travertine ceiling like blessings. The Strand was a place
where I could create my own dream architecture
while waiting for the movie to start, launching imagination
from the building's seven-story tiled façade, the mezzanine
studded with medallions, a chilled-air microcosm of
Sealtest Ice Cream and Coca-Cola,
Jane Fonda's atomic hairdo,
Yogi and Boo Boo in a helicopter surveying Jellystone.
Between the time our mom dropped us off
and picked us up, the theater was a space to
build a kid's fantasies of standing on the Juliet balcony,
dreaming myself into scripts,
constructing systems of play inside my head.
The theater closed early on its last night in the seventies, with no one
showing up to see a double feature of *Jeremiah Johnson* and
The Macintosh Man. The next day fire took it down to the ground.

BREAKFAST WITH MY SISTER

In a hotel restaurant, she brings her daughter,
my niece: a high school junior, college scholarship contender,

and local pageant winner. Tall and blonde, my sister was the family beauty.
I always wanted to present you to a man, as a prize, I remember

our mother saying to Vickie on one of her tears, while we all thought,
That's it, that's what's wrong, she just said it out loud.

Why has it taken me decades to understand? Older than I am by five years,
my sister remembers more. The names of their lawyers. My mother a victim,

not a monster, begging my father, *Can't we go somewhere besides Verdigre,*
his parents' farm, the seemingly endless drive

through Northeast Nebraska, little towns with false storefronts,
cafes with pressed tin ceilings, empty gazebos in empty parks.

We laugh about the time Vickie threw a chair through the picture window
of the old house, angry at age twelve, left alone to babysit four siblings,

and she tells me, *I went to the neighbors to call Child Protection Services.*
When her daughter asks why, she says, *I was sick of them leaving us alone*

all the time. I've told you before about my father putting us in the trailer
in Marie's driveway so they could be together in her house,

but my sister remembers it better. *I couldn't breathe,*
the air was pressing in on me. Didn't you feel it?

I was asleep, I tell her. *They put Dad in handcuffs,* she says.
What do you think they finally gave him? A slap on the wrist, a warning.

Why didn't we just open the door? she asks, and I'm stunned
that it never occurred to us. I think again of the time, many years later,

when my car was stolen in front of me, got stopped in traffic,
and I grabbed the handle of the passenger door. The thief knew what to do:

he zipped through the parking lot, me trotting alongside, until he cut away
down a side street. I want to be like him.

MY MOTHER BELIEVED IN CHRISTMAS

If my mother did not believe in the food pyramid,
orthodontia, and sobriety, she believed in Christmas.
If my father mailed me a check, my mother
read the Sunday supplement from Holiday,
the gas station on Thirteenth where I would later buy
my first album, by Creedence Clearwater Revival,
and choose a present from the wall of shelves
stocked with Fisher Price imitations
of the accoutrement of maturity. Faux radio,
sham television, and phony telephone
whose jangly ring disappointed with a null receiver.
Were they homage to or mockery of adulthood,
the narrowing in of perception,
items limited only to their intentions,
when what I loved were the clash of colors—
powder-blue handle against snow cone–
white body, sunburst-yellow speaker—
the hollowness and stiffness of inflated plastic,
and the slight hint of formaldehyde?

My mother believed in Christmas presents
just as she believed in staying home sick,
eating what you want, and watching television.
If my father believed in Chevrolets,
she believed in Fords.
If he believed in Nixon,
she believed in McGovern.
They both believed in
"stationary disease"—
their code name for laziness—
and cigarette smoke
as a cure
for
ear-
ache.

THE COUNCIL BLUFFS DRIVE-IN THEATER

The blue corrugated back of the screen
matched the parabola roof that sheltered
the ticket box. We piled in my dad's big Chevy
to see a movie, arriving at dusk,
playing on the swing sets below the screen,
the rhythmic rush of being pushed outward
to kick at the audience of anonymous cars
before falling backward, like a second thought,
waiting until dark so the movie could start.
What possessed my parents to take us to an R-rated movie?
Maybe we took what we got at the drive-in, whatever
was showing, and no one asked questions if
a blue-collar family with underage kids
rolled in to see *Bonnie and Clyde*. I was six years old
and remember an extended scene playing out
on the screen of a shootout punctuated
by the close-up of a hand with a finger missing.
And that's it. My attention was more focused
on the scene within the car, on soda bubbles clinging
to the edge of the circle atop a waxed paper cup,
on the heavy face of the electronic speaker,
its spiral neck tethered to a post beyond my father
in the driver's seat, my mother on the passenger side,
and my three sisters and me playing in the back,
how the drive-in made us both outside and in
at the same time, an inkling that home comes with you,
while the miracle of a soundtrack piped into the car
makes you notice the weight of every
simple action long after the movie is over,
the slide of soles on a step, the click of a key
in the lock, and the door opening to the glow
of a light above the kitchen sink.

BEQUEST

Aunt Mary Anne gave me two brown finches in a cage. These were my pets in fifth grade. I was ten. The cage sat on top of my bedroom dresser. The birds were round, companionable, and identical. I didn't know their sex. Usually they sat next to each other on the rung in the middle of their cage. It was fall, the air was gray, the trees were black. My mother had turned forty that spring. Before and after her birthday, she walked through the house with the corners of her face downturned. It was the seventies. She thought this was the end. Maybe it was. I remember her saying to Aunt Mary Anne, *I don't need men.* Mary Anne, also a big-boned divorcée, worked her whole adult life at the same job, as a sales clerk at Walgreens at the Crossroads Mall. Before the finches, she had given me a single blue fighting fish. I kept him alone in a round aquarium, blue gravel on the bottom, a green castle to swim through. Periodically he'd cover the water surface with clear, empty bubbles for an absent female fish to fill with eggs. I felt bad that he went to all this work for nothing, that his body needed something he couldn't control that no one nearby could supply. He lived his fishy life until he died of old age. But that cold autumn the birds got sick; their taupe bellies, their stippled brown wings, and their solid brown caps puffed out as their bodies chilled. I paced the house as I had seen my mother do before. My bird book said nothing about how to treat illness. Although I fed them regularly, the only thing I could think to do was to give them more. I asked for money so I could walk to Ed's Rexall Drugs on Tenth Street and buy a fresh box of Hertz birdseed. My mother said, almost more concerned than annoyed, *The way you are worrying you are acting like you're gay.* Then she gave me the money, and I walked the five blocks in cold twilight, bought the food, and fed it to the birds. They died overnight.

QUADRANTS OF THE BODY

I believe the body is a continent,
with the occasional skirmish of the leg,
a reconstitution of the skin,
a revolution in the blood.
During the divorce, my mother sang,

It's impossible.

In junior high my body held the line
of flag football when Jeff Simms
caught the ball and rushed left.
Charging me, growing larger
as a function of perspective.

Please release me.

Can the brain gain weight?
When I was six my father
handed me a lit firecracker
with no explanation
on the Fourth of July.

Make the world go away.

No keys to hang, I bought
rabbits' feet at the drugstore
in pink, green, and blue.
In heaven
all of my pets come back.

It's not unusual.

"AN OCEAN POURING INTO AN ABYSS"

I loved this book in grad school,
a Facts on File almanac
of the Wonders of the Natural World. In Brazil,
three million gallons of water plummet
three hundred feet every second
in the 275 individual falls of Iguaçu Falls.
What does a waterfall look like from above?
A brown drip-glaze plate, or the circle of a latte.
The once taut coil of yin and yang now sprung.
The erratic trail of an insect's life under bark.
Myth and physics free to commingle.
The placid surface of the head
belies the furious pounding
of the pistons underneath.
Viewed from below, the waterfall is only
the desperate, expansive gestures of the spray
in a perpetual state of panic.
From the side, the many falls, some falling into other falls,
are many little doors—I thought—
opening into the side of something big—
I didn't know what, an epistemology, hermeneutics—
a body of water so turgid it is still.
Restless myself, maybe I just wanted to believe
I could find a simple secret of the world in a book,
something about how the body works, or age, or time—
such as, to build is also to degrade.
Or maybe I just wanted to give myself some advice,
like, muddle through the middle
and make some noise at the end.

FILM ART

"Everything is not possible at all times."
—*Heinrich Wölfflin, quoted in*
David Bordwell & Kristin Thompson, Film Art

A teacher myself now, I couldn't tell you
the professor's or even the class's name,
but *Film Art* was my favorite text in college.

The globby inch-by-inch-and-a-half photos
in black and white, figures 1.1 to 10.29,
and a paltry color insert referenced every movie

I couldn't wait to see. My research
sends me back, remembering the importance
of deep focus, how a mirror in the mise-en-scène

doubled the space, extending the action
into the audience, or how a film was divided
into scenes by dissolves to black,

and how I had never noticed before.
The book lays out a reasoned approach to art,
distinguishing plot from story,

elements from conventions. Too high-strung
back then, I couldn't follow the diegesis
of any real-life situation, placing one moment

in the context of the previous and the next,
but film, like literature, is cumulative,
and the ending changes our perception.

The text lays out history in a comforting way,
from the horrors of Buñuel to the calm reframing
of three people at a table in a Hollywood picture.

The *New Wave* meant Godard and Truffaut,
who idolized auteurs like Hitchcock and Preminger.
It did not mean the Talking Heads,

my professor joked. In the eighties,
the fifties looked more modern than the sixties,
at least comparing chic Jean Seberg

in *Bonjour Tristesse* to the color-saturated hippies
of *La Chinoise* and *Daisies*. Today the opposite
is true. The book rolls it all together,

and I loved its serious, in-depth analyses of
Meet Me in St. Louis and *Swing Time*.
"For a few years, sound created a setback

for Hollywood film style." The camera motor
was picked up by the microphone, as was
the hum of mercury vapor and arc lamps.

So this is what age is, the buzz of anxiety,
a phase in which the noise of operation is evident.
I wish there were theaters around the world

showing every movie all the time.

Dolores in the office, middle-aged, dating a married man. We tried to talk her out of it. Like she had time to meet someone better. Getting hers while she could. Sometimes she would hug me out of the blue. She'd ask, *You don't mind?* I won't begrudge anyone her pleasure if no one gets hurt. We only live so long. Josette, the stray cat in our basement. I read online how to satisfy a cat in heat. Insert a Q-tip in the vagina. Lots of posts about what to do if the cotton swab comes off inside. The average life-span of indoor cats is eight to fifteen. Outdoors, just three to five. The grave is a fine and private place. Mom and Derf fucking in the living room. Made stupid by desire. At least she got hers before cancer winged her away from here. On Netflix, Andy watches the sixties' TV series *Voyage to the Bottom of the Sea*, comparing the hotness of the men. I worked in a mom-and-pop grocery store the year between high school and college. Except it was pop and pop. A married guy and his fat gay brother. Once I saw him naked in the storeroom, wiggling his gut on a vibrating-belt machine. The low sack of his balls shaking. Freddy Mercury sang "Crazy Little Thing Called Love" on the AM radio. Now and then, a stooped old man walked through the store, mumbling. Patty, the pretty clerk, told me what he was saying: *Soft young boys, soft young boys, soft young boys.* Once Patty visited my apartment. Her confused face after seeing a dress hanging in my bathroom, knowing I lived alone. It's usually the ones who are *not* obvious who end up hurting people. In junior high, drunk, asleep in Kevin's room, him naked next to me. Or sitting in the field at Bancroft, him rubbing his dick in front of me. On Eleventh Street to downtown, he asked, *What if I took off all my clothes and walked naked next to you?* Get yours while you can. Stop waiting. Pick up your hands.

THE CITY OF THE FUTURE

There are two kinds of people in the world: those who live above the horizon and those who live below it.

Let's pin our hopes on the blond boy in a speedo fighting a muscle-bound frog in a sub-Atlantic lair. He has swum so far to get here. Below sea level, it is revealed to us that communication is a matter of wires, waves, and hoses. Travel is a matter of wings or fins or flippers. When a puffer fish floats like a balloon in the sky, we know something is wrong.

There are two kinds of people in the world: frogs and ostriches.

We can learn so much from ostriches. When to look down our noses. When to bury our heads, the architecture of asses, the flowers of assholes. The Cold War is an economic engine. Remember, whatever you do, the big ostrich is watching. She is the fire that floats our balloon, the truck whose exhaust outlines our dream cities.

There are two kinds of people in the world: frogs and ostriches, puffer fish and squirrels, bees and flying horses.

Long ago in our history, back when we were stick figures crudely drawn, a frog led us to peace. She stilled the sword-waving hordes. She plugged the great volcano. Dinosaurs were granted another era to live. So we know it can be done.

When a puffer fish floats like a balloon in the sky, we know something is wrong.

Or is it? This is the land of transformations. To pee is to cry is to come. A frog becomes a bee. A man becomes an ostrich. A dog becomes a bird. A mouse becomes a truck. A totem becomes a dick. In an alternate universe, a garden of penises blossoms under a grow light. "My goodness there's some large tallywackers in there." A vagina is a cactus is a dress with fringe is a crow shitting is a pair of prosthetic legs is a tongue and a sponge is a carpet of hearts.

The city of the future is built of transparent super-towers, as thin as needles.

While a boob rolls by like a tumbleweed, the frog leader demands that we all recover. A war is fought with signs and banners. A volley of assertions. A bulwark of denials. What are we fighting for? For words and ideas. For signs and symbols. For English and Esperanto. For Nomi Malone in *Goddess*. For sludge fudge. For a lady with lorgnette. Her silence speaks volumes.

And this time, we didn't forget the gravy.

When a squirrel forces gravy down the maw of a frog, the frog defecates honey that feeds Pegasus and pelicans. A feathered dog is surrounded by frog cherubim, like Bouguereau's *Return of Spring*. There's something symbiotic about these frogs and birds. Thanks to them, the world keeps on ending, but never the same way twice.

"I was their plaything and their idol, and something
better—their child, the innocent and helpless creature
bestowed on them by Heaven, whom to bring up to good,
and whose future lot it was in their hands to direct
to happiness or misery, according as they fulfilled
their duties towards me."
— *Mary Wollstonecraft Shelley,* Frankenstein

Living in the gut of a machine,
we are raised by invisible corporations.
The greatest good for the greatest number.

Who does the counting?
Today is the anniversary of the abandonment
of an American city, a bureaucracy of errors.

Lacking the confidence of the medium's familiar,
the ghost in training devotes herself instead
to a scientific study of evil.

Good luck. Using the sense of touch,
I want to find Miss Isabella's springer Fanny
lynched with a kerchief on the moors.

Victor gives life to his monster
but denies him the right to pursue happiness,
so the monster deprives Victor of both.

Evil is a face as familiar as Ingrid Bergman's,
the senator from Colorado told us. Without asking,
everyone knows Heathcliff lynched the dog.

Wordsworth can't help me here.
Take me to the Northwest Passage,
the illusory amplitude of white.

COMING HOME AFTER TEACHING A CHAUCER CLASS IN WHICH I TOLD THE STUDENTS THE WIFE OF BATH IS A HUGE DRAG QUEEN

Occasionally history takes a wrong turn,
leaving banks of time to be erased
by our latter selves. Today, in unofficial tribute to the seventies,
I'm drinking Red Zinger, fondly remembering flairs and body shirts,
toasting my professors, who were themselves the students of
    D. W. Robertson,
founder of exegetical criticism. The purring of a cat
is the engine of the house I share now with my husband,
the heart of the organism that is marriage.

Chaucer's pilgrims *quit* each other,
one story answering another. Feudalism's
treasured hierarchy dims in the background, while
millers, reeves, and wives negotiate in the foreground
to keep community running.

Even the provisional homes of the past
deserve their due, answers
to a problem not of their making. After an ancient breakup, a nap
on the foldout sofa, home from teaching freshman composition.
A canopy of maples outside the apartment window
flooding the room with gold shadow.
The couple next door readying for bed naked
after a hard day's work, the curtains left carelessly open
across the narrow breezeway.

Revolution is followed by reaction
is followed by revolution. *This is fortune's wheel,*
I tell the students. My professors, who made the good society
a country I could visit comfortably,
urged me into law school during the Reagan recession.
I dropped out after a semester. This is mine to profess:
Art means so much more to me than money, and
I woot best where wryngeth me my sho.

BIRD, BATH, AND BEYOND

We hear it before our afternoon nap,
A scratching in the walls

Like mice scurrying
Or a phantom branch

Dragging in the wind two stories up
Where no trees reach.

From outside we see
A shingle has fallen away,

Exposing the opening
For an old stove pipe,

Dead-ended by plaster
On the inside. A bird

Has made her nest
In the hole in the wall,

A cliff dweller bathed in
Sunlight more generous than any

Cast in last July. From below
We see her beak protruding

From the tall plane of shingles,
Her profile's bob and jerk

As she holds sentinel.
Back inside, we rest

Our heads against the plaster,
The bird in the wall.

Beyond October, it is hard to say
If safety will remain in unlikely places,

But in our hearts
We hope it will.

THE PAST USED TO BE UNLIVED

I.
In the Haymarket, at the dairy's factory,
our job was to climb a stepladder to dump
expired milk from single cartons
into a giant carton.
The stench was foul, biological, familiar.
We didn't ask why we had to do this.
We assumed that like belongs with like.

II.
The foreman told me to move an ancient truck
from the lot to the loading dock.
Once in her new Honda Civic DX
my sister had tried and failed
to teach me how to drive a stick.
The day I had to do it on my own,
I pressed the clutch and shifted gears.

III.
Riding shotgun in a semi's open cab,
I jumped out when the driver paused at a curb,
the engine pumping and exhaling,
carried cast-off furniture
into the truck that residents had dumped,
and hopped back in the cab before he roared away.
One day was not enough to pick it all up.

IV.
The field boss called at 5:00 a.m., and I went
to the grain silos near the railroad tracks south of town.
Men younger and healthier than I lifted themselves
by their palms over the retaining wall to the open vats
of wheat. Our job was to break up the crusted surface,
thirty degrees hotter than the day's temperature, with shovels.
Blind, pink families of mice saw sunlight for the first time.

V.

When the agent would not reveal the work entailed,
I showed up anyway at the campus maintenance facility
with two undergraduates stranded in town that summer.
The superintendent lowered us into a cistern,
gave us gloves, masks, and putty knives,
and told us to scrape crude oil off the walls.
I climbed out and drove home.

VI.

My summer job in high school was working as a clerk
at Second Chance Antiques in the Old Market.
I hung Maxfield Parrish prints, bought an Art Deco
tie with my employee discount, and watched *Casablanca*
at the nearby revival theater. Back then
the past was another country I could visit. Today
it is an almanac of possibilities.

THE BIJOU

Walking from my apartment to the Bijou
at the University of Iowa Memorial Union in Iowa City
was like stepping into a wood-block print,
the black outlines of the street grid
containing the darkening lawns of the Pentacrest
and the Old Capitol, the sky dotted with stars.
Awkward and alone in a college town,
I found a safe place to be with people in the Bijou.
Standing in the nondescript lobby
among a crowd waiting for *Seven Sinners* to start,
I began to choke up until someone friendly
tugged my coat sleeve and said, *Here, you sit next to me.*
When Marlene Dietrich walked on stage in top hat and tails
to sing to John Wayne, the movie audience applauded.

Doris Day, her hair combed back in a ducktail, made John Raitt
wear the other half of her pajamas. Barbara Stanwyck
in *Ball of Fire* needed a cold compress after getting flushed
while kissing Gary Cooper. The man and the woman in the
cuckoo clock walked together into the same door at the end of
The Awful Truth. When Gregory Peck showed up at the lunch table
in *Spellbound,* the college audience gasped at his handsomeness.

From Jimmy Stewart I learned how to qualify a statement,
from Irene Dunne how to undercut a situation,
from Henry Fonda how to whisper in an ear.
The Bijou was the start of me taking care of myself,
just like the smart-talking dames and wisecracking mugs in the movies.
Walking home afterward was like moving a piece
forward on a board game,
the city blocks richly colored squares.

ANOTHER MAN'S POISON

It's easier to move in the dark.
This black-and-white movie is brown and gray.
A triangle of dots means stars through a window.
A revolving spiral indicates fire in the hearth.
The doctor is an actor and an author.
Pull the drapes and the waves of the lake are the lines of a paragraph.
Fury has to have his exercise.
England is an island, but the moors cover the world.
This man is another man.
The real husband plays the fake husband.
Bette Davis plays Bette Davis.
Moonlight is her sunlight.
Her eyes are two white opals set in the sides of her head.
She fusses with the nimbus of her hair.
This woman's not afraid.
This man has disgracefully long eyelashes.
She wants him.
While the young lovers talk downstairs, the old haters tussle upstairs.
When Bette gets mad, the camera gives us 360 degrees of fury.
Pull the drapes and the waves of the lake are eyes moving across the page.
Rain is strings of light hanging down the windowpanes.
The sky is bands of brown and gray.
The rain outside the doorway is dots of light.
A pretty question deserves an ugly answer.

STOLEN FACE

I am also on the other side of you.
Because you could not have me,

You made me, or a copy.
We are both practitioners:

You, a plastic surgeon;
Me, a concert pianist.

You created my face on another woman
And married her.

Your operating table is my eighty-eight.
My music is your respirator.

While I play my way across the continent
Your instruments whir and flash

Like centuries. Underneath the skin
Of beauty are hammers and strings,

Pedals and dampers. Before her surgery,
You made a sculpture of her face,

My face. Now, hers is hollow,
Broken on the floor.

Mine is a hood
Concealing pistons and blades.

SELF-PORTRAIT: A CENTO

I was admitted to three different hospitals—sanitariums, if you prefer—over a period of six years. I had a total of thirty-two electric-shock treatments. So there is hope for everybody.

Before the play we rode to "21" in a glistening new Rolls-Royce Silver Cloud.

The time on camera was less than one would like. And who wants to play a painting?

But try this: once I gained twenty pounds in a matter of weeks on a diet that consisted of bread and butter sandwiches and candy bars. I imagined I was pregnant and I was eating for two. Each night I would give birth, and each morning the Communists would steal my child.

In fact, it should be said that I have no recollection of some of the incidents described in this book.

Listen, you are with an old New York working girl, and there are other ways to get to the theatre besides a cab. Follow me.

MANIFEST DESTINY

Melvyn Douglas's nose
is an isosceles triangle.
Myrna Loy's Art Deco face
is echoed in the plaster busts
placed about her office. Business
flows through her veins.
Lies are her linguistics.

I can easily picture
Depression-era audiences
admiring her dexterity
as she prevaricates fluidly.
The Mrs. in front of her name
is job security. The absentee
husband is imaginary,

just like the movies,
corporations, nations, marriage,
or anything that pretends
to join or divide us.
Two by two and one by one.
We die alone, says
the justice of the peace.

Hollywood is New York.
America is one big city.
The big city is America.
Her hat is a basket of cherries.
In her décolleté are squash blossoms.
Her hair is heaped high
like a foxglove.

Her story is in his mind.
It tells itself. She invented
a husband, and he gave it to her.
She's the woman's head
on a man's body.
He's the man's head
on a woman's body.

The anima and animus
are gryphons, mermaids,
satyrs, windigos.
I can't tell which of them is me.
Even if I have not seen
this movie before,
I have seen this movie before.

Niagara Falls is the Grand Canyon,
the Grand Canyon is Niagara Falls.
He's from Wapakoneta,
Ohio, a Shawnee name.
Sitting on her lapel
is the turtle that holds
the world on its back.

LUCY GALLANT

Technicolor mellowed to the warm tones of a fairy tale.
The bedtime story of a fifties melodrama told in montage.
A boomtown jiggles within the dark frame of a windshield.
An oil rig surfaces through the steep escarpment of Heston's profile.
The alabaster menhir of Wyman's head
delivers snark through the ivory coliseum of her smile.
Eyes blinking, she nods a benediction at her fall.
Shall we postpone the overthrow until after the festivities?
We communicate in catchphrases. Lucy, they've coldcocked you.
Poor is rich. Oil is fashion. Hate is love. Texas is New York,
no, Texas is the world. Velvet from France, wool from Canada,
organdy from Switzerland, blue fox from Norway.
Edith Head's narration strides to climax: embroidered in Spanish jet,
the gown of Texas, with all the iridescent colors of oil.

HYPNOTISM IS A RELIGION TO ME

Her rooms on Angel Court
are scented with Clair de Lune.
Her reflection doubles on the surface,

one up, one down,
a face card, the Queen of Diamonds,
before she sends the lotus spinning.

Outside is the omnibus of London.
Men in granite overcoats.
The normative voice of our narrator

dissects the methodology of the detective.
He considers a severed human finger
no more potent than a rabbit's foot for luck.

The detective and the murderer
toast each other at a nightclub.
You have not found one clue.

A friend likes burning things.
Toy boats were my special joy.
Anything I could set afloat.

THE WRECK OF BEAUTY

On the border between perspective and knowing,
distracted by the geometry of Janet Leigh's sweater,
it's easy to miss the time bomb in the trunk.

As the camera floats more gracefully than God
over the tops of buildings, the promise of the grid
is infinity. We trust the city continues beyond our seeing,

I mean, the black-toothed horizon that stands for the city
continues beyond our seeing. At least one set of lovers
is going to die. That's the story.

We accept that Charlton Heston is Mexican
in the way that *red* stands for
what sunlight looks like through closed eyelids,

or that gangland is fairyland,
where the detectives rub shoulders like sex.
The lovers in the car that explodes could just as easily be

the lovers on the street who watch as the car explodes.
Janet Leigh suffers in the motel of memory.
Crossing the border, we know we don't know anything.

Ambivalence results when desire outlives the body,
or is it when ideas outgrow their words?
Marlene Dietrich's beauty runs down her face,

turning into something without a name.
I think she's getting ready to be done.
All she wants is a room-shaped room.

LADIES THEY TALK ABOUT

They say I'm beautiful, so I am.

It's how I'm cast. Warner Brothers

needed an actress who could play tough,

so I cracked wise while walking on a treadmill,

arms akimbo, before a prison-yard back projection.

It's what the era wanted—a heart-shaped face,

bow lips, and bobbed hair. When the movie

opens, I'm cheekbones glowing in the dark

of a phone booth. This is the studio at its grittiest,

in pre-Code Hollywood, when they knew

there were two kinds of people in the world,

gun molls and radio evangelists. We need both.

Once in a while those two get tangled up

and we have ourselves a story.

So this is the beginning. I still remember

that feeling of joy, that sense of promise

in the offing, having something to expect.

I didn't know then that happiness would not be

in what I'd get, but in the looking forward.

This is when my acting was closest to real,

"natural," they said, when my flip remarks

cut deep, and my screams were articulate,

when I could still remember the pain of my father

leaving to work on the Panama Canal,

and the hope I carried that he'd return

long after they finished building it.

BANJO ON MY KNEE

Thanksgiving on my stomach in the Santa Susanas
turns out to be the best way to cope with barbecued steak.

Will Rogers said to Clark Gable, *They will always make
more people, but they can't make any more land.*

When we are young, we dream of pleasure,
and we'll do anything, even trade our youth, to get it.

I could have pulled a blanket of words over my head
and hid underneath, the way I've seen others do,

divorced from their experience. Instead, I decided
to skip over this century of wars and genocide

and connect to what's real, get back to the earth.
Why not summon something from left field,

Gable and Lombard painting my fence, twenty barns
for twenty horses, a picnic with the stars?

Time to practice the fine art of decision-making.
Instead of choosing one moment from the next,

let's only use the present tense, with no inflections.
No more déjà vu or jamais vu. Bill Mulholland knows

Shangri La requires a lot of sacrifice,
and all I care about is work. I willed Marwyck into being.

The bare-boned trees we trucked in from the north
still smell of snow. We've planted them among the chaparral.

I'm glad I knew to live while I was still alive.
If I could die and come back, I'd be a star all over.

THE SHADOWGRAPH

Let's stand behind a white screen
and throw our clothes off at the audience.
If they wear special glasses

they can see us in three dimensions.
If they don't wear special glasses,
they can see nothing.

When we look back, we're embarrassed
by what we've put on film,
stories we would have forgotten

if we had not made them up.
Let's shoot the sequence over—
just show us as we really are.

Our naturalness outlasts
any implausible script—a gangster's moll
becomes a prairie pioneer,

Flatbush becomes the Great Plains,
the twentieth century becomes
the nineteenth—all in the course of day.

Somewhere in between,
Ruby Stevens stands naked and alone
in a frontier bedroom,

and the movie suddenly becomes real.
When we look through our special glasses,
we see Marwyck on the horizon,

a work-around for consciousness,
a home inside the head, devoid of meanness,
where every moment always happens.

SCREWBALL

After she drops an apple on the head of a brewery heir,
she dashes into a brownstone on the Upper West Side,

wearing rhinestones and fringe. The professor puts her
on a stack of books and sizes her up. She falls for the big lug,

but a gangster whisks her down to Jersey to get married.
She pretends to be a perfect housewife, but "Cuddles"

really does all the cooking. On Christmas Eve, her baby boy
becomes a baby girl, then everyone breaks into a square dance.

In a beaded gown and a mink coat, she leads her society pals
on a scavenger hunt through the Lower East Side,

where they stumble onto a crime scene. After a montage
of neon signs and champagne glasses, she unmasks the murderer,

who turns out to be "Cuddles." They all sit down to play cards
with a marked deck, as she targets her patsy in her compact

mirror. He is really more interested in a promotion and a raise
than in being her husband, so she smashes his favorite figurine

on the hearthside. She puts on a riding jacket and affects
an English accent. While the brewery heir stares at her legs,

the professor crashes through the door and punches the gangster
in the nose. She finally admits she loves him, the big lug.

NIGHT NURSE

In 1973 Barbara Stanwyck won the Wrangler Award
from the National Cowboy Hall of Fame.
Children are like cows. There are good ones
and there are bad ones. You can kill bad cows,
but you can't kill bad kids, she said to a reporter

after her estranged son Dion was arrested for selling pornography
to minors when his unemployment benefits ran out.
In pre-Code *Night Nurse*, she saves two children
from a doctor starving them to death for their inheritance
while their mother drinks herself under the table.

By the end of the marriage, my father and my stepmother
left us a gallon can of syrup, a loaf of white bread,
and a box of Jell-O. I poured the syrup on the bread
and ate it like a sandwich. I mixed water with the Jell-O
and drank it like orange juice. Stanwyck sent Dion

to private schools. She shipped him off for summer
to her mother-in-law's farm near Beatrice, Nebraska.
Before Dion went into the army he had lunch with Stanwyck.
As politely as a stranger I asked about her career.
As politely as a movie star she answered.

When he got married, she sent him a bedroom set.
A dresser, a bedframe, two nightstands, a vanity.
I love that little vignette. This mirror is for forgiving.
When I look in it, I see whomever I remember.
In 1981 an intruder in a ski mask woke Stanwyck up in bed.

He struck her across the face and stole her jewelry.
You can't afford to be too conceited.
If you do, you portray the West badly,
and you do the West an injustice. The West
was tough, hell-country, full of fights and wrongs and hardness.

Once, awake late at night, I felt the spirit of a big man, no one I knew,
coming at me fast out of the dark, and when I looked up
he didn't disappear so much as step aside. I wasn't frightened.
Ghosts have as much right to live as we do. But I don't want
to spend my death among the living. I'd rather be in Marwyck.

UNION PACIFIC

"Golden Spike Monument, S. 21st St. & 9th Ave.
This 56-foot golden concrete spike was erected in 1939
with the premiere of the film *Union Pacific*."
— *Council Bluffs Convention & Visitors Center Guide*

Stanwyck visited my hometown in 1939.
In the Great Depression, the age of breadlines,

there was a parade instead to Eppley Airfield.
In the age of hoboes hopping trains,

two freight cars full of klieg lights came instead,
and a façade was built downtown to look like 1860,

when the ceremonial spike of gold was
tapped into the ground to mark the linking

of the East to the West, nowhere near here, but in Utah.
However, Union Pacific's headquarters is in Omaha,

so that's where they had the premiere. That sounds
like my hometown: money talks, even when there isn't any.

On some grade school field trip in the sixties, I think
I saw a replica in the Union Pacific offices,

ensconced in a cube of plexiglass. On opening night in '39,
three theaters screened the movie simultaneously:

the Orpheum, the Omaha, the Paramount.
I remember when they all were still open,

palaces of marble, tile, and plaster, the streets lit gold
in the evening rain on some rare night my parents took us out.

Decades before I was born, Stanwyck waved to throngs—
some dressed in period costume (encouraged by the studio)—

at Union Station, an Art Deco treasure,
the same empty shell I walked past on my way to work.

Because we were ignored, anything could happen here.
The scion of the department store lived on the top floor,

surrounded by Native American art and big-game trophies.
Among the ghosts of buffalo and passenger pigeons,

who would pound a golden spike into the dirt?
Now the real one is in a museum in California.

In the era of the wpa Art Recovery Project,
Hollywood built a concrete obelisk painted gold

as a promotional gimmick for Cecil B. DeMille,
across the river in Council Bluffs. Decades later,

the Chamber of Commerce lists it in the *Visitor's Guide*.
So what? All that matters is Stanwyck was here.

If I had been alive and met her, I would have felt like
Tennessee Williams: "Stanwyck was gracious

and laconic; very tiny; very chic; very controlled.
But I met her! I saw the eyes, the lips. Contact was made."

STELLA DALLAS

Anne Shirley, who plays the daughter,
grew up on the RKO lot,
graduated from the studio high school.
For her eighteenth birthday,
Goldwyn gave her a car.
Hollywood was her every day.
She'd put in her shift on the sound stage,
then go home and cry
because the director would not direct her.
In *Stella Dallas* the daughter marries money.
Even though we know real life
is always about the young and sexy,
this movie is all about the mother.

Bird-breasted and *built for speed*,
Stanwyck wore three sets of stockings
in order to have thick ankles. She said,
It was a matter of upholstery
She stuffed cotton in her cheeks for jowls.
My poor old mom took it on the chin.
My dad dropped her when his first love
became available again. My sister remembers
more than I do: how our stepmother
walked the hall on Sunday mornings,
saying, *Your mother is a whore*,
saying, *You will all wind up in hell*.
My sister says she's buried now
in my father's hometown, that hag.

Anne Shirley played the younger Stanwyck
in *So Big*. If the daughter is the mother,
is she a premonition or nostalgia?
My sister's middle name is Anne,
in honor of our mother's mother.
Really, I have just a handful of memories.

The burgers at the café in Underwood
where my father took us. My sister
remembers the name of the place. I just
remember the taste of too much pepper.
Or walking my father's farm after school,
finding cacti growing in a stream bed.
Chasing the planter behind my father's tractor.
My sister says it's time to let that handful go
because it all comes down to dirt.

They say Stanwyck came from nothing,
even though her family dates back to 1740.
Her father left them to work on the Panama Canal
after her mother died. Her sister raised her.
Stanwyck's husband, Robert Taylor,
was born in a small town in Nebraska,
just like my father. During the making
of all those movies we love her for,
Stanwyck was suing the studios to get paid,
angry and grief-stricken at the loss of her sister.
In both the silent and the sound
versions of *Stella Dallas*,
at the end the camera closes up
on the mother crying at the fence,
as the story struggles to make sense.

NO MAN OF HER OWN

Null is both none and all,
the snake eating its tail.

No man may be every man,
or at least any man,

let's say, the brother of the dead.
Dumped by her cheating boyfriend,

a pregnant woman takes a train
to nowhere, which, again,

is everywhere, or anywhere,
looping in a circle or sphere

into infinity. After a crash
we all become someone else

anyway, so why not make the most
of it? The world is the cast.

She takes the place of a dead lady
and goes home to her family.

Is it wrong to fall in love
with the brother?

Too old to play this part,
she looks for something lost.

Even if she found it now,
what we know

and can remember is the feeling
of being lost, of missing

something, so that even
after it's found, we keep looking.

TO PLEASE A LADY

Why would you need to take care of her?
    The catcalls on the racetrack are her due.
Barbara Stanwyck is in drag as a newspaper columnist.
    Middle-aged sex emanates from her epaulets.
Clark Gable in a mini-speedster is her die-cut toy.

The stadium lights shed moondust on the tracks
    while a spotlight catches in the lens,
a dotted line cuts diagonally across the frame.
    The crowd clamors for blood but is silent
when they get it. She understands he was in it to win.

His head is a cement block that squarely rides the barrel
    of his chest. Her honey contralto goes staccato,
setting the pace for his raspy twang.
    Her retinue is in service to sensation.
She writes scandal while trying on shoes.

When a woman fucks a man on-screen,
    her cheekbones grow higher,
her eyes spread even wider. The effect of glamour
    on a nice Irish girl from Flatbush.
Gable drives through flames as hot as history.

His face twitches involuntarily from the war,
    a skull and crossbones emblazoned on his shirt.
He crashes through ice as thick as the Russian front.
    This is the unwilled part of our inheritance.
The Ferris wheel turns against a starless sky.

Let's stop the poem while she's still ahead.
    In life Barbara always called the shots,
sleeping with women as well as men, dropping dreamy
    Robert Taylor's ass when he fooled around.
He was only worth a couple of lies.

THERE'S ALWAYS TOMORROW

The father is neglected by the family.
The son doesn't care about him until he's discovered in the desert,
laughing with Barbara Stanwyck in the bungalow of lust.
For that, he gets a pompadoured sneer,
a toy robot walking off the edge of a table,
a single plane flying over the broken I of California.

Joan Bennett looks great in a low-cut dress.
I wear the same style, and I'm no ingénue myself.
Fred MacMurray is here on a business trip
with Stanwyck, two trim figures in swimsuits emerging from a pool.
*After twenty years of marriage
a husband doesn't rave about anything.*

Let's skip the second act and go to your office, Stanwyck tells MacMurray.
Work is more appealing than fun.
Playing is an industry. Outside the beveled window,
the manufacturing plant chugs and smokes.
In the showroom, the stillness of the dolls is stultifying.

The gingham check of light and shadow covers the floor.
The outlines of two middle-aged lovers swell
behind frosted glass as they approach the door.
The shadow of rain slides down Stanwyck's face.
A room divider splits MacMurray into stripes.

At the hotel, the contents of her purse spill across a smoked mirror tabletop.
MacMurray thumbs a torn photo of himself.
*Someone snapped it of us at the annual picnic.
I cut myself out of it because I looked so ghastly.*
A desk is a bed where the image of the self lies down.
*I want to look pretty. Not for attracting boys,
but for the sake of my dancing career.* Part of love is work.

The son must stop the father from having any fun. It's his occupation.
Joan Bennett is impervious to passion.
The bedroom's overhead light fixture witnesses the couple's desperation.
Stanwyck's cheekbones and shoulder blades are chevrons,
but her voice is all business. Let's go outside to look inside.
The leaves are petrified. Beyond the patio, Los Angeles shivers.

MELODRAMA

Act I

A woman is alone in a room in a city.
Her room is in a skyscraper.
The windows are outsized,
and the view is important.

Her hair is carefully disheveled
or tightly coiffed.
She has an air of professionalism
or an air of desperation.

She knows a dangerous secret.
Either no one will believe her
or she won't admit it to herself.
A stranger tries to convince her

or her husband tries to tell her
that it's all in her head.
She slowly begins to believe him.
She furiously refuses to believe him.

The phone rings multiple times
She answers it and shudders.
She answers it and screams.
Someone is outside the window.

Act II

She stumbles to him in her nightgown.
She spies on him through binoculars.
He is Sigmund Freud,
playing a shell game.

She has to guess which cup hides the coin.
He is Adolf Hitler,
holding a puppy.
She has to entice the dog away from him.

They end up going to court over custody
of the dog.
Hitler's lawyer, Joe McCarthy,
subpoenas her deceased parents.

Freud dons a snood and a pencil skirt
to masquerade as her mother.
Hitler testifies
that he's her real father.

The judge commits her to a sanitarium.
Still alive, she is put in an open casket
and given shock treatment.
The dog is run over by a car.

Act III

She falls in love with her doctor.
He discovers she has a terminal disease
without a name. She will be pretty
until the day she dies. Snow will fall

outside the window on that day.
But before then, the doctor's
children disapprove of their romance,
so she breaks up with him.

He releases her from the sanitarium,
and she walks in the middle of the street,
her shoulder pads backlit by the sun,
never to see him again.

Then her husband reveals he is the stranger,
Hitler, and Freud rolled into one,
and he is the one who ran over the dog.
He chases her into a skyscraper.

They climb endless flights of stairs.
When he charges toward her at the top
she dodges, and he spirals to the pavement.
The little dog limps into her arms.

WITNESS TO MURDER

How are you supposed to know

what they tell you without words?

Once you translate one sign,

how many more require decoding?

No one believes you except

the murderer himself. Listen

without telling. Their memory

is just as good as yours.

After you witness him strangle a girl,

George Saunders's insinuating tone

places you in a mental hospital

for the old and lonely. Everyone

hates you there, they say.

You come out rehabilitated, conditioned,

until you let the mask drop

and name what you are seeing,

call the murderer a murderer.

Once we face the fact,

what else do we have to admit?

Once you find out you were right,

what does that mean

for every other instance of doubt?

THE NIGHT WALKER

On the arm of fashion designer Nolan Miller at the 1974 Academy Awards,
it's a long way from the Ziegfeld Follies or the Strand Roof,
dancing with the Keep Kool Cuties.

Forgotten, too, the scandal of "Hollywood's Unmarried Husbands and Wives,"
which forced Barbara Stanwyck and Robert Taylor
to make it legal.

The days of Sugarpuss O'Shea, her hair all doozied up, are gone.
Tell Ralph Edwards and *This Is Your Life* she'll take a powder.
Tell Richard Avedon to fuck off.

In the divorce decree, she stuck Taylor with paying her fifteen percent
of his gross earnings for the rest of his life.
She never remarried.

At Hollywood parties, she was the tallest person in the room,
even sitting down. But just like us, she was waiting
for an opportunity to leave.

She knew the world moved on without her. The crew still called her Queen
or Missy, but after age fifty
you slip to second billing.

So when William Castle offered her *The Night Walker* costarring Taylor,
she said, *You better ask Bob.* He said,
It's as if we were never married.

We may assume, now, all that's left of the diegesis is for the two old sinners
to do a postmortem together
outside the limelight.

What becomes a legend most? Four glasses of water in the morning.
A big, hearty breakfast. A breeze through the window.
Not to have to talk to anyone.

A MAP OF THE STARS

A map should be a reason. Like a transcript
of an argument, there should be some logic to it,
some explanation as to why the hills abut the valley,

the young forget the old. I was never good at thinking
my way into the future, so let's houseclean the past
instead. For $2.00 you get a map of the stars' homes.

Trace the coordinates from the index, A to M horizontally,
1 to 8 vertically, and you can put your finger on me.
So many things I wanted to do, and now there's time.

Sometimes I watch myself on television,
the *Late, Late Show*, but they've cut my movies
all to bits, so they don't make sense anymore.

In *The Other Love* they chopped the end off;
I give a deathbed speech then break to a commercial,
never to come back, making me look like I am crazy,

always dying, never dead. The map uses asterisks
to denote the former homes of stars—
here's where Judy Garland used to live,

here's where Carole Lombard used to live. The message
of the map is: death is a metaphor, the image lives on.
Our decisions are directions, an algorithm of identities:

here is your face lit from below by the dashboard,
here is your face broken by the arrows of an iron fence.
We all become our own audience at the end.

So when I opened the front door to get the newspaper
and my stalker jumped out, *I'm here, I love you, baby*,
I didn't waste any time bringing him up on charges.

The judge sent him to Atascadero State Hospital,
but before he could be designated as a sex offender
he went to trial and served as his own lawyer.

I took the stand and testified, but the jury ruled against me.
Afterward, he kept on stalking me. I found him sleeping
in my garden. I caught him cutting through my screen door.

I moved to a different house just to get away.
The movie star who played tough broads and
wisecracking dames with a chip on her shoulder

was as weak and as vulnerable as anyone in the audience.
The map should tell us: the shock is not in knowing
what we've lost, but in realizing what we never had at all.

WALK ON THE WILD SIDE

A person must play a character.
Sometimes the character is too close to home.
I played a lesbian madam in *A Walk on the Wild Side*,
even though I turned down Margo in *All About Eve*.

I had always played women of appetite.
I knew my companion Helen Ferguson would not be offended.
She of all people knew Bob and I were a lavender couple.
I didn't need to reassure her.

Does saying "I'm sorry" really make a difference?
Forgiving those I've harmed is easy after they are gone.
When war broke out, I threw myself into service,
but I was no hero; there was more I could have done.

After the war, when McCarthy rose to power,
I played along in his rank attempt to kill the New Deal,
to rout FDR's liberal intellectuals and gays.
I sent Bob to testify. He was the first star to name names.

And then I continued to work with those he named.
You wouldn't think it, but I was broken up
when he left me for another woman.
It wasn't the end of Camelot exactly.

Ava Gardner wasn't Guinevere and Bob wasn't Lancelot,
unless Lancelot was queer.
But after that, the world just kept on ending.
Those who remember are cowed, diminished, chastened.

We made the mistake of putting the heart before the course.
What's left is doing the same thing over and over.
During the height of the studio system
I was freelance. Sometimes I liked working better than living.

Working was a way to shut down thinking.
Once we start remembering we also start forgetting.
A person must go back to the beginning of the ending
to find the invention of solitude.

THE FURIES

When Walter Huston wrestles a calf
out of the mud in Anthony Mann's

The Furies, while Barbara Stanwyck
throws back her head and laughs,

it's the most honest image in Hollywood.
Our feelings are a blast of music.

Love and lust are blam, blam, blam.
1950 hated the world for not being pretty.

When Stanwyck casts aside pearls
for diamonds, it changes the air

in the theater. When she rides her horse
to the squatter's fort

and warns her Mexican lover,
she wrings the neck of eloquence.

You'd think the happiest answer
would be transposing an old-world

problem to the new. But Utopia
doesn't last here either.

Stanwyck doesn't like what they've done
with her image, the myth of the West,

taken from the Golden Age to Iron. It's funny
how they think it's theirs,

when she knows it's hers.
Mann saw the pretty in the ugly.

Sometimes winning is just outliving.
Even God is not above the body.

TITANIC

Living a decade in, a decade out of an arduous century,
I've seen enough of suffering.

Trussed up in a lifeboat on a Hollywood set,
forty-seven feet above

a tank of roiling water, extras in their lifeboats
tossed about below me,

I surrender to great racking sobs over loss in our time,
within our living memory;

how different today would be if the ship hadn't sunk.
That's why I built Marwyck, a young woman's folly,

some place safe from the cracked-up hull of humanity.
Brittle stalks of grass by a dry creek bed.

The sweet acidic crush of juniper berries. We can taste it,
but we can't live there forever.

After a few years I sold my interest in the horse ranch
to the Marxes and rented a house with Bob.

Now that he's gone he's closer than ever.
When I clutch my Oscar, he speaks to me.

The dead ask us to forget the endings. They request
we take a reasoned approach to remembering.

Scenes fade out. That's the nature of scenes.
What matters is that somewhere in the Sierra Nevada

a herd of wild mustangs, mares and foals,
stands on a mountaintop, hissing steam, pawing the snow.

SORRY, WRONG NUMBER

Sometimes the lines get crossed.
You think you're in one conversation
but then you find out you're in another.

Something about worry is addictive.
Once you start feeling it, you want to perform it,
like it's a religious rite. As the lies repeat,

they become the truth.
Even after they are gone, they are still there.
In her mind, Leona was sick,

and that was enough to make her body sick.
She performed the rite of lying in bed
wearing a lace nightgown, berating her husband.

Being a bitch is really being a weakling.
Spending worry before bad things happen
makes you broke when they do.

Your responses become conditioned.
That's how you end up agreeing to things
in court that you don't really agree with.

It's like not fighting on the playground.
Or letting a stranger push you against a fence.
Sometimes the process takes over, and you sign off.

Just taking it, like you've been trained.
Don't get out of the bed, don't go scream
out the window, don't try to save your life.

DOUBLE INDEMNITY

If your lipstick smears, the makeup man will fix it.
That's his job. We all have jobs.
Don't teach me, help me.

Stand still while centuries move around you.
You try not to age, but sometimes it's unavoidable.
With every role, you grow another skin.

If you're going to practice making decisions,
you'll need to be able to change your mind.
It's what the script calls for.

Maybe you didn't know at the time
you were in the right place. The way they lit the set,
the moves, the business, the atmosphere,

made it easy for you to slip into your role,
to see your hand on the banister, the bracelet on your ankle.
All you ask is to appear in the last fifteen minutes,

your face in multiples around you.
If you are the watcher and the watched,
then you must be in every movie ever seen.

As the filming wraps, you think, *I hope she'll be okay.*
You miss people before they are gone.
Sometimes, when you talk to yourself, you answer, *Yes, me too.*

ACKNOWLEDGMENTS

Thanks to the editors of the journals and anthologies in which some of the poems in *The Shadowgraph* previously appeared, sometimes in different forms:

The Adroit Journal: "Saturday Night"
American Society: What Poets See, edited by Robert S. King (FutureCycle Press, 2012): "August 29"
The Blue Earth Review: "Bird, Bath, and Beyond"
Bloom: "Coming Home after Teaching a Chaucer Class in Which I Told the Students the Wife of Bath Is a Huge Drag Queen"
The Fourth River: "An Age at Least to Every Part"
The Freshwater Review: "Self-Portrait: A Cento"
Main Street Rag: "Double Indemnity" and "Ladies They Talk About"
The Newport Review: "The Past Used to Be Unlived"
Nimrod: "Stella Dallas"
The North American Review: "Hypnotism Is a Religion to Me"
Oakwood: "Titanic"
Poetry City, USA: "The City of the Future"
Queer Voices: Poetry, Prose, and Pride, edited by Andrea Jenkins, John Medeiros, and Lisa Marie Brimmer (Minnesota State Historical Society Press, 2019): "Double Indemnity," "Melodrama," and "The Furies"
Smartish Pace: "Marwyck"
Soundings: "An Ocean Pouring into an Abyss" and "Union Pacific"
Superstition Review: "Bequest"
Switched-On Gutenberg: "Quadrants of the Body"
The Threepenny Review: "Retrospective"
UCity Review: "A Map of the Stars," "Manifest Destiny," "No Man of Her Own," "There's Always Tomorrow," "To Please a Lady," "Sorry, Wrong Number," "Walk on the Wild Side," and "The Wreck of Beauty"
Valparaiso Poetry Review: "The Council Bluffs Drive-In Theater"
Water~Stone Review: "Breakfast with my Sister"
Whistling Fire: "My Mother Believed in Christmas"

I'm grateful to the Minnesota State Arts Board for an Individual Artist's Fellowship in Poetry while writing this manuscript.

Thanks to my writing group—Christopher Tradowsky, William Reichard, and Greg Hewett—for encouraging me to write movie poems. This book is dedicated to my sisters Vikki, Rita, and Julie, and to my late mother, Kathleen, for their example and inspiration.

My thanks to everyone at the University of New Mexico Press, including Alexandra Hoff for her eagle eye in copyediting, Katherine White for her savvy marketing and publicity, James Ayers for his skillful project management, and Mindy Basinger Hill for the beautiful cover design and page typesetting. My deepest gratitude to Elise McHugh for believing in this book, and my highest respect and admiration to Hilda Raz for her wisdom, guidance, and support.

Finally, my eternal thanks and love to my husband, William Reichard.

NOTES

"An Ocean Pouring into an Abyss": Rupert O. Matthews, *The Atlas of Natural Wonders*, Facts on File, 1988.

Film Art: David Bordwell & Kristin Thompson, *Film Art,* Addison Wesley, 1979.

An Age at Least to Every Part: "An age at least to every part," Andrew Marvell, "To His Coy Mistress."

The City of the Future: This poem was written in response to a collaborative art exhibit, Ekphrastic, at Soo Visual Arts Collective Gallery, Minneapolis, Minnesota, and was performed there on June 4, 2016. The quote in the fourth stanza is from Heid E. Erdrich. Thanks to Megan Vossler and Carolyn Payne at SooVAC for organizing the exhibit.

August 29: The date Hurricane Katrina made landfall near New Orleans as well as the birth and death dates of film actress Ingrid Bergman.

Another Man's Poison: *Another Man's Poison*, starring Bette Davis and Gary Merrill, directed by Irving Rapper, United Artists, 1951.

Stolen Face: *Stolen Face*, starring Paul Henreid and Lizabeth Scott, directed by Terence Fisher, Hammer Films, 1952.

Self-Portrait: A Cento: All lines in this poem are from Gene Tierney with Mickey Herskowitz, *Self-Portrait*, Wyden Books, 1979.

Manifest Destiny: *Third Finger, Left Hand*, starring Melvin Douglas and Myrna Loy, directed by Robert Z. Leonard, Metro-Goldwyn-Mayer, 1940.

Lucy Gallant: *Lucy Gallant*, starring Jane Wyman and Charlton Heston, directed by Robert Parrish, Paramount, 1955.

Hypnotism Is a Religion to Me: *The Woman in Green*, starring Basil Rathbone and Nigel Bruce, directed by Roy William Neill, Universal, 1945.

The Wreck of Beauty: *Touch of Evil*, starring Charlton Heston and Marlene Dietrich, directed by Orson Welles, Universal, 1958.

Ladies They Talk About: *Ladies They Talk About*, starring Barbara Stanwyck and Preston Foster, directed by Howard Bretherton and William Keighley, Warner Brothers, 1933.

The Shadowgraph: In the Ziegfeld Follies in the 1920s, young Barbara Stanwyck performed in a piece called the Shadowgraph, where she stood behind a screen topless; the audience was given polaroid lenses to enhance the 3-D effect. *The Purchase Price*, starring Barbara Stanwyck and George Brent, Warner Brothers, 1932.

Banjo on My Knee: *Banjo on My Knee*, starring Barbara Stanwyck and Joel McCrea, directed by John Cromwell, Twentieth Century Fox, 1936.

Night Nurse: *Night Nurse*, starring Barbara Stanwyck and Clark Gable, directed by William A. Wellman, Warner Brothers, 1931.

Union Pacific: *Union Pacific*, starring Barbara Stanwyck and Joel McCrea, directed by Cecil B. DeMille, Paramount, 1939. This poem ends with an excerpt from a quote by Tennessee Williams that is used as one of the epigraphs for Victoria Wilson's *A Life of Barbara Stanwyck: Steel-True, 1907–1940*.

Stella Dallas: *Stella Dallas*, starring Barbara Stanwyck and Anne Shirley, directed by King Vidor, United Artists, 1937.

No Man of Her Own: *No Man of Her Own*, starring Barbara Stanwyck and John Lund, directed by Mitchell Leisen, Paramount, 1950.

There's Always Tomorrow: *There's Always Tomorrow*, starring Barbara Stanwyck and Fred MacMurray, directed by Douglas Sirk, Universal, 1956.

To Please a Lady: *To Please a Lady*, starring Barbara Stanwyck and Clark Gable, directed by Clarence Brown, Metro-Goldwyn-Mayer, 1950.

Witness to Murder: *Witness to Murder*, starring Barbara Stanwyck and George Saunders, directed by Roy Rowland, United Artists, 1954.

The Night Walker: *The Night Walker*, starring Barbara Stanwyck and Robert Taylor, directed by William Castle, Universal, 1964.

Walk on the Wild Side: *Walk on the Wild Side*, starring Barbara Stanwyck and Jane Fonda, directed by Edward Dmytryk, Columbia, 1962.

The Furies: *The Furies*, starring Barbara Stanwyck and Walter Huston, directed by Anthony Mann, Paramount, 1950. This poem is for Greg Hewett, whose great uncle, Thomas Gomez, also stars in the movie.

Titanic: *Titanic*, starring Barbara Stanwyck and Cliffton Webb, directed by Jean Negulesco, Twentieth Century Fox, 1953.

Sorry, Wrong Number: *Sorry, Wrong Number*, starring Barbara Stanwyck and Burt Lancaster, directed by Anatole Litvak, Paramount, 1948.

Double Indemnity: *Double Indemnity*, starring Barbara Stanwyck and Fred MacMurray, directed by Billy Wilder, Paramount, 1944.

BIBLIOGRAPHY

Callahan, Dan. *Barbara Stanwyck: The Miracle Woman.* Jackson: University
   Press of Mississippi, 2012.
D'Orio, Al. *Barbara Stanwyck: A Biography.* New York: Coward-McCann, 1983.
Klevan, Andrew. *Barbara Stanwyck.* London: British Film Institute, 2013.
Madsen, Axel. *Stanwyck.* New York: Harper-Collins, 1994.
Smith, Ella. *Starring Miss Barbara Stanwyck.* New York: Crown, 1974.
Vermilye, Jerry. *Barbara Stanwyck.* New York: Pyramid, 1975.
Wilson, Victoria. *A Life of Barbara Stanwyck: Steel-True, 1907–1940.*
   New York: Simon & Shuster, 2015.